# Ruth Handler:

## I Created Barbie™

T0390205

*Thomas Kingsley Troupe*

**Mitchell Lane**
PUBLISHERS

## Parent and Caregiver Tips for Creating Nonfiction Readers

The high-interest topics in the *Who Am I?* series are sure to get your young reader excited about reading nonfiction. While exploring a fascinating subject, your reader will be introduced to new concepts, facts, ideas, and vocabulary.

## Tips for Reading Nonfiction

### Talk about Nonfiction
Explain that nonfiction books provide facts about real-world topics. When readers read nonfiction, they gain a rich understanding of the world. They build background knowledge that provides a foundation for learning and academic success.

### Look at the Parts
This book contains the following helpful features. Share the purpose of each feature with your reader.

#### Photos, Captions, and Graphic Aids
The photos, captions, maps, diagrams, time lines, and other graphic aids in nonfiction texts contain a wealth of information. Help your reader identify different ways information can be displayed.

#### Sidebars
These extra tidbits of information help satisfy readers' curiosity and expand their knowledge.

#### Table of Contents
Located at the front of the book, this list shows the big ideas within the text and the page numbers where they can be found.

#### Glossary
Located at the back of the book, the glossary defines key words and phrases that are related to the topic. These words and phrases can be found in the text in colored type.

#### Comprehension Questions (Fact Check)
Multiple-choice questions help readers self-check to make sure they understand what they read.

#### Index
Located at the back of the book, the index is an alphabetical list of topics and the page numbers where they can be found.

With a little help and guidance, your reader will be on their way to enjoying and learning from nonfiction books.

## Mitchell Lane

### PUBLISHERS

### mitchelllanepub.com

2001 SW 31st Avenue
Hallandale, FL 33009

First Edition, 2025.
Author: Thomas Kingsley Troupe
Designer: Rhea Magaro
Editor: Kim Thompson

Series: Who Am I?
Title: Ruth Handler: I Created Barbie / by Thomas Kingsley Troupe
Hallandale, FL : Mitchell Lane Publishers, [2025]

Library bound ISBN: 979-8-89260-251-8
Paperback ISBN: 979-8-89260-440-6
eBook ISBN: 979-8-89260-260-0

PHOTO CREDITS
Alamy: MediaPunch Inc, cover, 1; Hum Historical, 9; Kohl-Illustration, 13; Underwood Archives, Inc, 18; Tsuni/USA, 23; Barbie: 16, 24; Matel: 4, 7, 19, 20, 21, 25, Newscom: Piero Oliosi/Polaris, 8; Shutterstock: Elena Ivan - Papadopoulou, cover, 1; rblfmr, 6; 8th.creator, 7; K I Photography, 10; 360b, 11; Gaia Conventi, 11; dragon_fang, 14; Sean Pavone, 15; JHVEPhoto, 22; Oxy_gen, 23; Romanchini, 27; Wikimedia: 15, 17

# Contents

# Rich and Famous

Over the years, she's had over 200 different careers. She has lived in more than 20 Dreamhouses. She drives fancy sports cars. Her closet holds over one billion outfits and accessories. Who is she? She's Barbie®!

Barbie's hair may be blond or blue. She might be wearing a lab coat or a ball gown in her **signature** shade of pink. No matter how she looks, the **iconic** doll is one of the most popular, collectible toys on the planet.

She may not look it, but Barbie is over 65 years old. Since 1959, Mattel® has been selling Barbie, her friends, and their clothes and accessories.

But dolls are only part of Barbie's world. There are Barbie books, games, TV shows, and music albums. Barbie is on watches, sleeping bags, lunch boxes, bicycles, and just about anything else you can think of. She has starred in more than 40 movies. The 2023 film *Barbie* was a hit around the world.

Where did the famous character come from? Who started all this?

### Creator Corner

Mattel claims that over 100 Barbie dolls are sold every minute. A Dreamhouse, Barbie's fabulous, multistory mansion, is sold every two minutes.

# Meet Ruth

Ruth Handler is the creator of Barbie. She was born Ruth Marianna Mosko on November 4, 1916, in Denver, Colorado. Her parents were **immigrants** from Russia. Ruth was the youngest of their 10 children. At the time Ruth was born, her mother was in poor health.

**Ruth Handler**

**Creator Corner**

In the early 1900s, many women did not have jobs outside the home. But Ruth's family taught her that women could lead businesses and make money.

When she was still a baby, Ruth went to live with her adult sister Sarah. Sarah and her husband ran a drugstore and soda fountain. Ruth liked to work there, and she became interested in business.

Ruth met Elliot Handler, an artist, when the two were in high school. They fell in love.

Ruth began college at the University of Denver. But during her sophomore year, she visited California and decided to stay. She got a job as a secretary at Paramount Studios in Los Angeles. Elliot moved to L.A. too. The couple married in 1938.

The Handlers liked to experiment with making things in their garage. At the time, new **plastics** were being invented. Elliot used Lucite® and Plexiglas® to make lamps and furniture. Ruth made business deals to sell the items. Along with a partner, Harold "Matt" Matson, they formed a company called Mattel in 1945.

### Creator Corner
The word *Mattel* is made up of letters from the two men's first names, Matt and Elliot. They did not include Ruth's name.

# The Birth of Barbie

Mattel began to make plastic toys. Their first big seller was a toy instrument, the Uke-a-Doodle. They made a toy gun called the Thunder Burp. A talking baby doll, Chatty Cathy, was a hit.

One day, Ruth watched her daughter Barbara play with paper dolls that represented different careers. She wondered if kids would play with a doll that wasn't a baby doll. Ruth thought a doll that looked like an adult woman might inspire girls. It might encourage them to imagine their future in different ways.

## Creator Corner

Barbie's full name is Barbara Millicent Roberts. She was named after Ruth's own daughter Barbara. Barbie's boyfriend, Ken, was named after Ruth's son.

13

Mattel's other partners didn't like Ruth's plan for a grown-up doll. But Ruth did not give up on her idea.

In 1956, Ruth went to Switzerland and saw Bild Lilli dolls. They looked like adult women, and they came with different outfits. Ruth was excited. She bought a few dozen Lillis and brought them back to the United States. Later, Mattel bought the company that made Bild Lilli dolls.

Using the European dolls for inspiration, Ruth developed her own adult fashion doll. It took three years to get it just right and to convince her partners at Mattel to give the idea a chance.

On March 9, 1959, Barbie made her **debut** at the North American International Toy Fair in New York City. The plastic doll was 11.5 inches (29 centimeters) tall. She wore a black-and-white swimsuit and came with shoes, sunglasses, and earrings. She cost three dollars.

# Barbie Mania

After Mattel aired a TV commercial for the doll, Barbies began to fly off store shelves. Over 300,000 sold in one year. More Barbie products followed. Barbie's boyfriend Ken was introduced in 1961, her best friend Midge in 1963, and her little sister Skipper in 1964.

**Creator Corner**
Released in 1992, Totally Hair Barbie was the bestselling Barbie ever. The doll had hair that reached her feet. More than 10 million were sold.

Through the decades, women's roles in **society** changed. Barbie changed too. More than 250 different Barbies have been made to show what women can do and be. Barbie has been a detective, pet groomer, doctor, robotics engineer, ambassador, beekeeper, train conductor, game show host, Air Force officer, race car driver, teacher, business executive, judge, architect, and presidential candidate.

Early Barbie dolls show a tall, thin, white woman. Over time, the Barbie brand became more **inclusive**. In 1980, the first black and Hispanic dolls called Barbie were released. Since then, Barbie dolls have represented many different races and ethnicities.

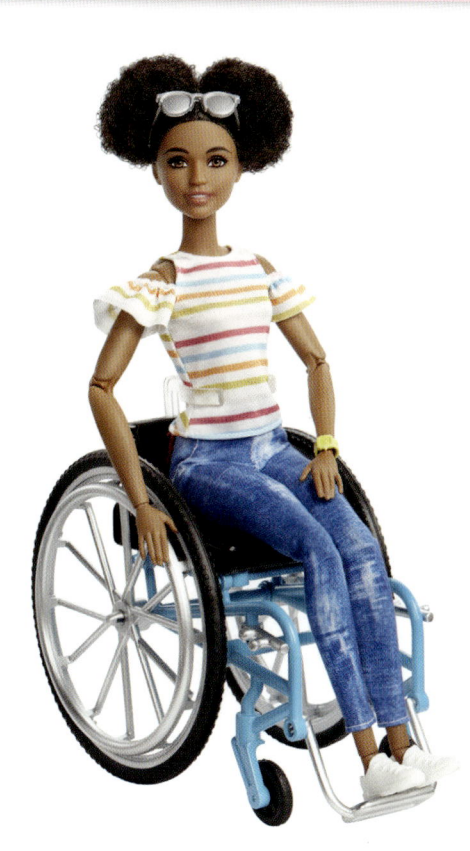

In 2015, people could buy Barbies with different heights and body shapes. Barbies showing physical disabilities came on the market in 2019. A 2023 Barbie was designed to represent people with Down syndrome. Today, Mattel says that its Barbies have 35 skin tones, 97 hairstyles, and nine body types. And more Barbies are being introduced all the time.

# Ruth's Truth

Ruth served as president of Mattel for nearly 30 years. She helped turn it into an incredibly successful business. In 1973, she and her husband left the company.

**Creator Corner**

Actor Rhea Perlman plays Ruth Handler in the 2023 live-action movie *Barbie*. She tells Barbie, "We mothers stand still so our daughters can look back and see how far they've come."

In 1970, Ruth learned she had breast cancer. After a **mastectomy**, she invented a product called Nearly Me to help breast cancer survivors feel more confident. To sell it, Ruth and business partner Peyton Massey formed a new company, Ruthton.

On April 27, 2002, Ruth Handler died during a surgery. She was 85 years old.

Ruth said the reason she created Barbie was to **empower** girls to dream big. "Don't take no for an answer," she said. "If you believe in something, keep pushing forward and never give up." Her message is alive today in Barbie's mission, which Mattel says is to "inspire the limitless potential in every girl."

The glamorous world of Barbie continues to delight millions of people worldwide. Ruth proved that with determination and creativity, everyone can achieve their dreams.

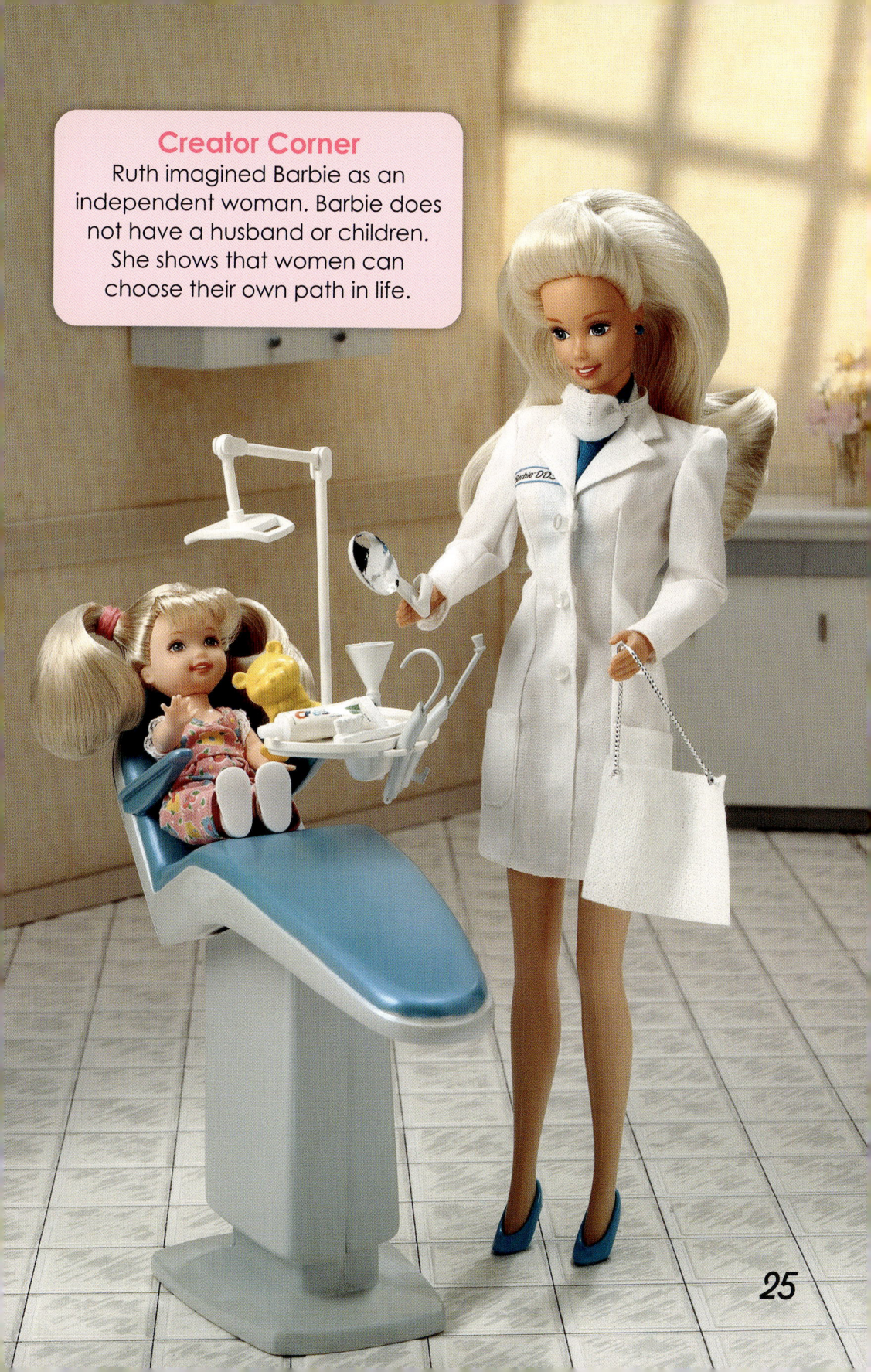

**Creator Corner**
Ruth imagined Barbie as an independent woman. Barbie does not have a husband or children. She shows that women can choose their own path in life.

# Be a Creator

Do you have the imagination to change the world like Ruth did? You do! Every big success begins with a small idea. Ruth watched her daughter playing with paper dolls and saw an opportunity. She wanted to create a more lifelike toy that would inspire kids.

Ruth was asked about her beginnings at Mattel. She said, "We didn't know how to run a business, but we had dreams and talent."

Design a toy that you and others would love to play with. What does it look like? How does it work? Sketch your ideas. Try to build a **prototype**. With hard work and determination, you'll invent an amazing toy!

# Time Line: Ruth Handler and Barbie

**1916** Ruth Marianna Mosko is born in Denver, Colorado.

**1932** Ruth meets Elliot Handler in high school.

**1938** Ruth marries Elliot and becomes his business partner.

**1945** The Mattel company is founded. Early products include lamps, picture frames, and dollhouse furniture.

**1956** On vacation in Switzerland, Ruth sees Bild Lilli dolls that look like adult women and that inspire her to develop a new fashion doll.

**1959** The first Barbie doll is presented at the North American International Toy Fair in New York City.

**1961** The Ken doll is first sold in stores.

**1965** A Barbie astronaut outfit is released four years before Neil Armstrong walks on the moon.

**1970** Ruth is diagnosed with breast cancer.

**1973** Ruth and Elliot Handler resign from their positions at Mattel.

**1976** Ruth starts the Ruthton Corporation to manufacture breast prosthetics called Nearly Me.

**1992** Totally Hair Barbie becomes Mattel's highest-selling doll of all time.

**2002** Ruth dies from surgical complications at the age of 85.

**2023** The live-action *Barbie* movie is released in theaters. Margot Robbie stars as Barbie, and Rhea Perlman plays Ruth.

# Glossary

**debut** (day-BYOO)
a first public appearance or performance

**empower** (em-POU-ur)
to give someone power, authority, or ability

**iconic** (eye-KAHN-ik)
widely recognized; classic

**immigrants** (IM-i-gruhntz)
people who move from one country to another to settle there, often to find better opportunities

**inclusive** (in-KLOO-siv)
welcoming to everyone, especially minority groups and people who have been discriminated against

**mastectomy** (ma-STEK-tuh-mee)
the surgical removal of the breasts, often to prevent the spread of cancer

**plastics** (PLAS-tiks)
light, strong, synthetic substances that can be molded into different shapes; cellophane, vinyl, Lucite, and Plexiglas are examples of plastics

**prototype** (PROH-tuh-tipe)
a test or original model of a product

**signature** (SIG-nuh-chur)
closely associated with someone or something

**society** (suh-SYE-i-tee)
the community of all people and the customs and traditions they share

# Fact Check

1. Ruth Handler got the idea for Barbie while watching her daughter play with _____.
   A. mansions       B. paper dolls       C. Hula-Hoops

2. Barbie's full name is _____.
   A. Barbie Marianna Handler
   B. Bernice Matilda Jones
   C. Barbara Millicent Roberts

3. Ruth found the Bild Lilli dolls that inspired Barbie while vacationing in _____.
   A. Switzerland     B. Egypt     C. Jamaica

4. Barbie was first shown to the world at the _____.
   A. Toy Box Symposium
   B. North American International Toy Fair
   C. Top Toy Flea Market

Answers: 1. B, 2. C, 3. A, 4. B

# Further Reading

Broeckel, Tara. *Female Force: Ruth Handler–Creator of Barbie*. Portland, OR: TidalWave Productions, 2023.

Eagan, Cindy. *The Story of Barbie and the Woman Who Created Her*. New York: Random House, 2023.

Slater, Lee. *Barbie: Ruth Handler (Toy Stories)*. Minneapolis, MN: Big Buddy Books, 2021.

# On the Internet

**Barbie**
https://kids.britannica.com/students/article/Barbie/638447
Read about Barbie's origins and her place in pop culture.

**Barbie: Fast Facts**
https://www.barbiemedia.com/about-barbie/fast-facts.html
Read amazing facts about the world of Barbie.

**Kiddle: Ruth Handler Facts for Kids**
https://kids.kiddle.co/Ruth_Handler
Learn more about the creator of Barbie.

# Index

# About the Author

Thomas Kingsley Troupe is the author of hundreds of books for kids. He never had Barbies of his own, but his cousins did. Teaming up with his G.I. Joe figures, they would go on action-packed adventures. Sometimes the army guy was the hero, and sometimes Barbie saved the day. When Thomas is not reading or writing, he's exercising, watching movies, traveling, or maybe taking a nap. He lives in Woodbury, Minnesota, with his two sons.